SWIMMING

BROWN

PHYSICAL EDUCATION ACTIVITIES SERIES

Edited by:
AILEENE LOCKHART
University of Southern California
Los Angeles, California

Evaluation Materials Editor:
JANE A. MOTT
Smith College
Northampton, Massachusetts

PHYSICAL EDUCATION
ACTIVITIES SERIES

SWIMMING

BETTY J. VICKERS
San Fernando Valley State College

WILLIAM J. VINCENT
San Fernando Valley State College

Illustrations by **BETTY J. VICKERS**
San Fernando Valley State College

WM. C. BROWN COMPANY PUBLISHERS
DUBUQUE, IOWA

Manufactured by WM. C. BROWN CO., INC., Dubuque, Iowa
Printed in U. S. A.

Preface

Swimming is a universally enjoyed, pleasurable activity. Its origins go back before any recorded history and no doubt many early men were accomplished swimmers. It is interesting and meaningful to note that one of the earliest published books was *The Art of Swimming* (1538).

This activity serves many purposes: men learn to swim to survive, to search for food, to improve physical handicaps and health in general, to become safe in a foreign environment, to become capable of participating in other aquatic activities, and to swim for fun. Regardless of your purpose the fundamental skills needed are the same. This little book was written to help speed your progress. Learn to swim well—respect the water—observe all precautions; if you do these things you will become safe and "at home" in the water and your enjoyment can be limitless.

Self-evaluation questions are distributed throughout these pages. These afford you typical examples of the kinds of understanding and levels of skill that you should be acquiring as you progress toward mastery of swimming. You should not only answer the printed questions but should pose additional ones as a self-check on learning. These evaluative materials are not necessarily positioned according to the presentation of given topics. In some instances you may find that you cannot respond fully and accurately to a question until you have read more extensively or have gained more experience. From time to time you should return to troublesome questions or to skill challenges until you are sure of the answers or have developed the skills called for, as the case may be.

Contents

What Swimming Is Like

Through the ages swimming has become an extremely popular as well as necessary skill. Once the fear of the water is removed most people experience a certain exhilarating feeling from submerging themselves. Perhaps this feeling results from the water's cooling effect on a hot day, but more likely it results from that unique feeling of weightlessness produced by the buoyant action of the water. Absence of the normal pull of gravity can have a relaxing and tension removing effect on your physical and mental state. For this reason, and for the wide recreational opportunities that the sport makes possible, thousands of people spend countless hours in swimming.

The primary purpose of learning to swim is to make oneself at least reasonably secure when in or near the water. For this reason alone, everyone should learn to swim. Age does not appear to be a limiting factor to learning, as children have been known to swim before they can walk and older folks use the water for its recreational and therapeutic values. In addition to the safety factors which are discussed later in this chapter, swimming offers keen enjoyment through unlimited recreational possibilities while concomitantly offering certain physiological and social values.

VALUES OF SWIMMING

Physiological Values—Our hearts, lungs, muscles and body systems need regular and vigorous exercise. Swimming contributes to the development and proper maintenance of most vital processes and few activities contribute as much to the development of physical fitness. Through swimming, most of the body's muscles are used, and by acting against the resistance of the water they gain strength. However, since swimming is primarily an endurance activity (the resistance is low but the repetition of movement is high) the cardiovascular system benefits perhaps more than the general muscular system.

The heart and vascular systems supply needed oxygen and nutriments to the body cells and carry away carbon dioxide and waste products. Maintaining a repeated activity such as a swimming stroke places a stress on this system which results in improvement of its ability to transport the materials in the blood stream. Through the use of floatation devices and by varying the amount of energy put into the stroke, you can regulate the extent of the strain put on your system and thus reap the benefits desired. Improvement in cardiovascular efficiency and the development of strength which results from moving against the resistance of the water is what is normally referred to as improving your physical fitness through swimming.

Recreational Values—Because of unprecedented advances in technology, science, medicine, and economics, man is fast approaching the point where he can turn more and more to increasing free time for fulfillment of creative self-expression. Knowing how to swim opens the door to countless recreational and leisure time activities. By learning how to swim, one can contribute to his present leisure needs while preparing himself for adventure in future aquatic activities.

It is no longer difficult to find facilities for most water sports. Billions of dollars are spent annually so that people can swim. Hotels, motels, resorts and other forms of commercial establishments feature swimming as a prime activity to attract people for a night, weekend or their entire vacation time, and soon there will be more than a million pools in this country.

Swimming opens up the frontier for new adventure and pleasure in the aquatic world. Recreational activities which one can enjoy after learning how to swim include competitive swimming, lifesaving and water safety methods, fancy diving, synchronized swimming, water shows, skin diving, SCUBA diving, surfboard riding, canoeing, motor boating, water skiing, sailing, fishing, and simple water games.

Social Values—Among the most important reasons for knowing how to swim are the social values that accrue. Swimming affords a splendid opportunity for youth and adults to participate together in healthy and natural aquatic activities. Because water sports are so diversified, many social groups in the form of aquatic clubs today are organizing and holding periodic meetings throughout the year for the purpose of competition and socialization. Swimming provides opportunities for the association of people from all parts of a community. It is one of the most popular family activities because it makes it possible for a family to play and recreate together. Through observing some of the unwritten laws of swimming (Chapter 8) certain social skills and courtesies can be developed and these may help you make new friends and enjoy your social activities to a greater extent.

Saftey Values—It has been estimated that 40 percent of all persons who are drowned yearly are school age children, and about half of these are engaged in nonswimming activities when drowning occurs. The safety values of being able to swim are of extreme importance. The ability to swim provides a great amount of insurance against possible mishap or tragedy.

For your own safety, as well as for the safety of your family and society, you should learn to swim. With the heavy increase in the number of aquatic facilities and equipment, both public and private, safety in and around water becomes a daily necessity. If you cannot swim it is extremely unwise to participate in aquatic activities. The ability to swim safely and the prudence to recognize and practice safety procedures are of prime importance to you. Some hints on how these can be accomplished are offered in Chapter 7.

Considerable time and effort are spent by the armed forces in an attempt to teach men and women to swim. Numerous lives were lost during recent wars by drownings. Many armed forces personnel were dumped in the water from amphibious landing craft during operations. In most cases the drownings which resulted could have been prevented if the men had been able to swim well, or in some instances were able simply to tread water. The most effective way of reducing the number of swimming accidents is to teach everyone to swim. Be a good and safe swimmer.

Special Values—Swimming is highly recommended by physicians for people with certain mental and physical disabilities. The buoyant force provided by the water allows a handicapped person to execute certain body movements that are impossible for him to perform otherwise. The handicapped person, the blind, the paralytic, the palsied, the crippled, and the injured person may find through swimming the assistance, the outlet, and the physical exercise so urgently needed for swift improvement and recovery.

Competitive Values—Man is naturally competitive. You probably like to see how you compare with your friends in the performance of certain

3

skills. Swimming offers you the opportunity to compete with others in many ways. Seeing who can swim the fastest or the farthest or with the best form, who can jump the highest off of the board, who can make the biggest splash or the funniest dive are games that are enjoyed by many. Such natural outlets to this competitive drive help you progress both physically and emotionally.

For those who desire even greater opportunity to compete, organized teams in schools and in private institutions are available. They are discussed further in Chapter 10.

EQUIPMENT AND FACILITIES

One of the aspects of swimming that makes it so universally enjoyable is the lack of expensive equipment. For more complicated activities such as water skiing and SCUBA diving, intricate equipment is necessary; but for a recreational swim all you need is a suit.

The suit can be obtained easily, but finding proper facilities that are both safe and sanitary may present a more difficult problem. In highly populated areas, public and private facilities are readily available to the interested participant. Just any old lake, stream or beach, however, may not be the best place to swim. Contaminated water, submerged rocks or treacherous currents may be present and such natural hazards should be thoroughly checked. But when these problems are eliminated, it is hard to top the pleasure of diving into the "old swimmin' hole."

2

Watermanship
Techniques
for the Nonswimmer

Perhaps the hardest part of learning to swim is getting over the initial fear of water. Stories are continuously repeated about how "I learned to swim because my Dad threw me in deep water and said 'sink or swim.'" Not only is this rarely completely true, but two undesirable consequences probably result from such an unwise method of learning. The person either sinks rather than swims or is left with a fear of water that may never be surmounted.

Not all people have an original fear of water. Indeed, some children have to be held back before they are safe near pools or oceans. Whether you are fearful or not, the best way to approach swimming for the first time is slowly and rationally with some time-honored techniques that are used by all well-qualified instructors.

GETTING USED TO THE WATER

Entering the Water—Your first contact with cold water may be somewhat of a shock. Swimming water usually is considerably colder than bath water, and contact with it causes several reactions. Probably the most common of these is the noticeable tenseness and tightening of your muscles. Your skin may shrivel up slightly and you may get "goose pimples." When you submerge to chest depth, your breathing becomes more difficult. This is due partly to the pressure of the water on the rib cage and partly to the tenseness of the musculature needed in breathing. In addition, you might notice a quickening of your pulse. The strange feeling of buoyancy also begins to take effect at this point. This·may produce a very exhilarating

5

feeling and can cause some laughter and desire to let yourself bob a little. Don't be afraid to let yourself go. Enjoy this feeling, for it is one of the unique things about swimming.

If the water seems too cold at first, don't go in all the way. Stand about knee deep and splash some water on your arms, trunk, neck and head. This will also help you become accustomed to the change in temperature and submersion will then not seem to be so drastic.

Relaxing in the Water—Once you are in the water, the next step is to feel relaxed in it. If you can find a spot where the water is only about two feet deep, sit on the bottom and let your feet float up in front of you. Keep your hands down to balance your new-found weightlessness and try moving around. Roll over from your back to your face and vice versa. Let the back of your head dip into the water while you keep your hands on the bottom, and then let your legs and trunk drift up into a float with your back almost parallel to the bottom. Turn over and try the same thing on your face.

Submerging—After you begin to feel relaxed in the water, try putting your head under water. Duck just a little at first so that your nose and mouth are submerged; hold your breath for a few seconds and come up. Next time let your whole head go beneath the surface, hold the position for a few seconds and then surface. Try to resist the temptation to wipe your eyes with your hands. This is a bad habit to get into for later on it will inhibit your progress. The water in which you are swimming is much cleaner than the water you drink from a faucet, so you do not have to worry about infection in your eyes. Some water will get in of course, but it will not hurt and you will get used to it. Later you will not even be aware of it.

The next time you go under, open your eyes slightly. The sight you see will be amazing. Other swimmers in brightly colored suits, the bottom of the pool and your own body, all in a blurry but beautiful scene, will greet your eyes. The blur results from the changed angle of refraction between water and your eyes which is different from that which occurs between the air and your eyes. Blur can be corrected by wearing a diving mask and you may want to try this. With it the same beautiful picture emerges but in crystal clarity. Imagine seeing fish, seaweed, shells and other sea life in this setting. No wonder skin and SCUBA diving have become so popular!

Have a partner or your instructor hold out several fingers under the water while you go down and count them, or drop some coins in the water and dive down to the bottom and pick them up. These two drills will demonstrate to you your ability to see under water and will help you in getting accustomed to your new environment. One caution about coins, however: don't leave them on the bottom for they will stain the pool. The same rule applies to hairpins and other metallic objects that rust.

Rhythmic Breathing—Once you have mastered the techniques outlined, you are ready to begin rhythmic breathing. Breath control—that ability to hold your breath and release it gradually or rapidly, to exhale, to gasp air or inhale quickly—is difficult to develop, and yet it is essential for maximum success in water activities. Nature did not endow man with the apparatus to convert the oxygen in water to suitable use for the body, consequently man will suffocate unless some adjustment is made. Diving tanks, aqua lungs, snorkles and the like have been developed to sustain man in and under water for long periods of time, but success in the use of such equipment and water activities not involving them depends upon your individual breath control.

Holding your breath is the first step. Take a deep breath and submerge; hold it for a few seconds and surface. The next time try counting to ten, then twenty, and finally thirty. When you reach forty-five, you have good breath control. You will find that thinking of something else while under water will make it easier to hold your breath.

Be certain that you do not try to stay under too long; one minute should be about maximum. If you find it difficult to keep yourself under the surface, "fin" by pressing toward the surface with the palms of your hands held out to your sides. This finning action is a simple press with your palms up and a recovery with your wrists relaxed. Your hands are drawn down the sides, and then pressed upward toward the surface, with your finger tips pointing out and away from your body. Repeat this action in a short, rapid rhythm.

Bobbing—Breath control is not limited to breath holding. You must develop the ability to breathe in and out according to the head actions of the stroke you are performing. The first rhythmic breathing method to practice is called bobbing. Begin learning bobbing by holding on to the side of the pool in about chest deep water. By bending your knees and straightening them, bob up and down holding your breath the whole time. Make the rhythm of the bob even and try to break the surface about every two seconds. After you have mastered this, take a breath of air, submerge and blow all of your air out in about two seconds. Then try it again; inhale, submerge and exhale so that it now takes five seconds to get it all out. Repeat this exercise varying the length of time you take to exhale completely so that you can do it at any rate required.

Now standing in chest deep water, combine the exhalation with a rapid inhalation. Assume the bobbing position, inhale, submerge, exhale and surface at the two second rate. Time your breathing so that you always exhale when you are under water and inhale when you are above. At first you will be able to make only about three or four cycles before you have to break the rhythm and take a few breaths above the surface, but keep practicing until you can go on indefinitely at your normal breathing rate with complete confidence and comfort.

Figure 1—Bobbing

While bobbing, don't be alarmed if some water enters your mouth. It will not go back beyond your tongue unless you swallow or suck it in while you inhale. Let it pool up in your cheeks or under your tongue and simply expel it with the next exhalation. One of the skills that has to be mastered in this bobbing technique is the separation of the air from the water in your mouth. This will come naturally with practice, so do not feel bad if you cannot do it perfectly at first. (Figure 1.)

Rhythmic Breathing for Swimming—You are now ready to begin developing rhythmic breath control for swimming strokes. Standing in waist deep water in a stride position, one leg forward and one leg back, hold on to the side of the pool and lean over so that your upper body is resting on the surface of the water. Extend the arm that is holding on to the wall and hold the other back or out to the side. Take a breath, place your face in

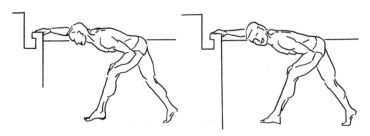

Figure 2—Rhythmic Breathing for Swimming

the water so that the water level is at your hairline and exhale. Turn your face to the side, away from the extended arm, just far enough to inhale through the mouth. Then turn the face back down and exhale through the mouth and nose. Continue this action, breathing rhythmically, as before. Keep your eyes open and your ear in the water while inhaling, and neither shake nor rub the water out of your eyes while you are practicing. This type of rhythmic breathing will be used later in the crawl stroke. (Figure 2.) (Refer to Chapter 2 for additional practice.)

Moving in the Water—So far all your techniques have been in a static position. To navigate properly, you must propel yourself through the water. Begin by walking in about waist deep water. Because of the density of the water, you will find that you cannot go very fast. Lean forward and draw your hands and arms back, as if separating a curtain of water before you, to help pull yourself through the water. Reach forward with both hands in front of you, then turn the palms and thumbs down and then out to pull your hands and forearms through the water sideways back to your hips. This is much like the breast stroke pull and this pull increases your speed in walking considerably. Experiment with your hands by pulling and pushing in various directions. Discover how to turn your body clockwise and counterclockwise with your hands. Jump and do a full pirouette and come down on your feet. If you happen to go under, surface again as you did in rhythmic breathing practice.

Now go into about chest deep water with a kickboard. Hold it out in front of you with both hands. Bend your knees and push forward slightly so that your feet come off the bottom and you are supported by only the board. Glide or float for a few seconds and then return your feet to the bottom. If your legs float up and won't come down, bend your knees and hips so that your knees come up under your chest and push down on the board while lifting your head, then extend your legs and feet straight toward the bottom and stand up.

Flutter Kicking—The kick that is used most often in swimming is the flutter kick. You can perfect it while holding onto the side of the pool. Place one hand on the gutter of the pool and the other against the side about one foot deep. Point the fingers of this hand down toward the bottom with the palm up against the side. By pulling with the top hand and pushing with the bottom one, raise your feet and legs up until they are parallel and just under the surface of the water. Begin kicking your whole leg up and down from the hip joint. Do not forcibly bend your knees or ankles. Keep them loose. When your leg kicks down the knee will bend from the water presure, and when you kick up it will straighten from the pressure.

How far can you swim under water: 5 feet, 15 feet, 25 feet?

Evaluation Questions

Emphasize the "up" phase of your kick in order to secure maximum speed and power. Later on you can forcibly extend your knee at the end of the

Figure 3—Flutter Kick Practice

down stroke, but at the beginning keep it loose so that you will develop the proper technique. Let the ankles stay as loose as possible and point your toes very slightly inward so that you feel a little pigeon-toed. Let the water flop your feet up and down like swim fins. Count your kicks in a six stroke rhythm. (Figure 3.)

While you are holding onto the side and kicking, practice your rhythmic breathing by turning your head sideways to inhale and down to exhale. Keep your head in a position so that the water level hits you at the hairline when you are exhaling, and have your ear submerged, with the water level just below the mouth, when you are inhaling. Add this rhythmic breathing and the flutter kick to your float or glide with the kickboard so that you propel yourself across the pool.

Swimming Under Water—Another skill that sounds hard but is really easy to learn is swimming under water. Once you have learned breath control, the flutter kick and the long breast stroke pull that was used in walking through the water, you are ready to swim under water. Stand with your back against the side of the pool and submerge. Put one foot up against the side of the pool, both hands stretched out in front of you, and push off into a prone position about two feet under the surface of the water.

10

Kick your feet up and down vigorously in a flutter kick and pull your hands and forearms back to your hips as before. You will probably go only about five or six feet the first time, but your distance may be increased by repeating the pull and kicking harder and faster. Open your eyes and count the lines on the bottom of the pool as you swim past them. (Figure 4.)

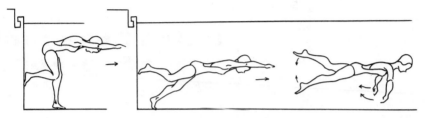

Figure 4—Underwater Swimming

All of the foregoing skills may be simple for you to learn, so progress at the rate which is comfortable for you. Do not go on to a new stage until one skill is accomplished, but move as fast as you can and listen to the hints and directions given by your teacher. Do not force yourself to attempt deep water stunts or other activities in which you do not feel prepared. Ask your instructor when you think you should progress to another skill and then follow his advice. When these basic skills have been accomplished you are ready to go on to regulation swimming strokes and techniques.

3

Skills Essential
for Everyone

Skills for swimming are varied and numerous; each swimmer must determine which of these is essential for him. You may find it necessary to learn each skill in a step-by-step progression in order to gain any success at all; others may completely omit many steps and yet demonstrate high competency. A well-rounded swimmer, however, familiarizes himself with each step and is accomplished in even the most simple basic movement.

FLOATING

The first essential skill is floating. Although the technique involved is somewhat natural to many, it is not to all. Everyone, however, can learn the skill either of motionless floating or of floating with minimal kicking and finning. There are three positions in which a person can float. The first is called the jellyfish; this type of float can best determine one's capacity to float. The prone or face float is the second type and is the beginning position for all strokes performed on the stomach or face. The third type of float is the supine or back float. Floating on the back is more difficult for most people but control in this position is an essential prerequisite to performance of all strokes done on the back. (Figure 5.)

Jellyfish Float—You should begin by working on the jellyfish float in the shallow end of the pool. Stand in chest deep water, take a deep breath, bend at the waist, place your face in the water while you slide your hands down your legs and grasp your ankles. This action should cause your feet to lift off the bottom of the pool; in this position your head, arms and legs will point down toward the bottom of the pool in a "jellyfish" position. To

Evaluation Questions

Can you float on your back 5 seconds? 30 seconds? 2 minutes?

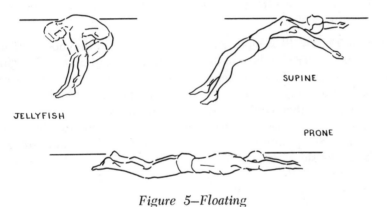

JELLYFISH

SUPINE

PRONE

Figure 5—Floating

return to a standing position, sweep your arms in a circular motion out to the sides and then down and forward; at the same time your knees, which were drawn up to your chest, are extended to stretch your feet to the bottom of the pool. Shake the water out of your eyes; do not rub them.

Prone Float—Once the jellyfish float is accomplished, the prone or face float becomes relatively easy. From a standing position in chest deep water, extend both arms out in front of the body and stoop until your shoulders are under water. Take a deep breath and place your face into the water. Lean gently forward and let your legs and feet come off the bottom of the pool. Don't push hard off the bottom of the pool, but allow the water to support your weight slowly. To stand up, draw your hands and arms back to your sides and down toward the bottom in a circular motion. At the same

13

Can you name two errors in this supine float position?

Evaluation Questions
ERRORS IN FLOATING

time, draw your knees to your chest and then extend your feet to the bottom of the pool.

Supine Float—The supine or back float is perhaps the most difficult to learn because water may be splashed over the face and nose and beginners often become tense when this happens. The use of noseclips while learning the back float and back strokes *may* be helpful, but their use should be discouraged because they could become habit forming.

Again, start by standing in chest deep water with one foot forward and one foot back. Stoop until the water is over your shoulders and extend your arms out to the sides at shoulder height. Take a deep breath and lay your head back in the water until your ears are submerged. Now lift your chest and allow your body to level off on your back. Keep your chest and stomach up. Do not sit in the water. Make no attempt to get your feet to the surface; most people will float in a semi-vertical position on their backs. You may need to extend your arms overhead to find a balance point, but be sure to keep them under water. If you had some trouble floating in the jellyfish position, you may need to scull by pressing out and in with your hands in a palms down position and/or kick slightly, but relax and try to hold this basic position for maximum floating effectiveness with minimum effort. (Figure 6.)

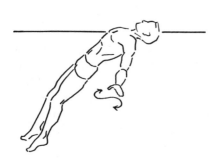

Figure 6—Supine Float and Scull

14

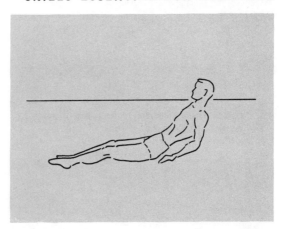

Diagram A:

ERRORS IN FLOATING

Balance is the main problem in the back float. Be sure that your arms are stretched well out to the side or well overhead as needed, and that your chest and stomach are held high. Scull or kick only if it is absolutely necessary. Try holding the back float without assistance. To return to a standing position, sit in the water by raising your head and dropping your hips. At the same time scoop your arms back and down in a circular motion and draw your knees to your chest. Then extend your feet toward the bottom.

SWIMMING ON THE SURFACE

Prone Float and Flutter Kick—The prone or face float and flutter kick is the first step toward learning swimming strokes. From the fully extended prone float position, the up and down flutter kick is added to propel the body across the pool. To do the flutter kick you should keep your legs relatively straight but relaxed, so there is some bend at the knee. The kick should be about eighteen inches deep and rather fast (about one complete revolution of the kick per second). Your legs move in an action similar to that in walking except that the ankles are extended. Your feet and legs should be kept under water throughout the kick with no more than your heel breaking the surface at any point. Greater flexibility in the ankle will produce a more powerful kick, provided all other aspects are correctly performed. (Review Chapter 2 for flutter kick practice.)

To add this kick to the prone float, extend your arms out in front of your body while you are standing in chest deep water with your shoulders under the surface. Take a deep breath and place your face in the water so that the water level is at your hairline, gently push off from the bottom into a prone position and kick from the hips—this action will propel your body across the water. It may be necessary to link your thumbs to keep

Can you flutter kick across the pool? Can you do it on your back as well as on your face?

Evaluation Questions

your hands together. Try to stretch your body in as long a line as possible for maximum success.

Supine Float and Flutter Kick—The supine or back float and flutter kick should be the first step toward learning strokes on your back, and it should be practiced early in the learning experience. Too often swimmers learn only prone swimming so the transition to other positions is difficult.

The flutter kick on the back is similar to the flutter kick on the face, with a strong emphasis of the up action of the kick. Again the legs should be kept relatively straight but relaxed with the toes and ankles extended. There should be some knee bend, and the kick should be deep and rather fast. Be sure not to sit in the water but to keep your trunk as straight and level as possible.

Adding the flutter kick to the back float is much like adding the kick to the face float. From a standing position in chest deep water, stoop to submerge your shoulders, extend your arms overhead and place your head and arms back in the water. Take a deep breath and gently push off the bottom into a supine float position, and kick from the hips, thus propelling your body across the pool.

Finning—The back float and flutter kick may be performed with your arms at the sides rather than overhead. The arms at the sides position is easier but the arms overhead position encourages a better body line for future stroke development. Until sufficient strength is developed it may be necessary for you to add a finning motion with your hands while working on this kick. Finning is performed by drawing your hands up at the sides of your body and then pushing the palms down toward the feet. It is an alternating press and release action. Both hands are drawn up simultaneously and the press results from a whipping action of your hands and forearms with your finger tips pointing out, thus the press is toward the feet and propels the body headfirst. Be sure to keep your eyes open and your breathing as regular as possible.

Turning Over from Prone to Supine Positions—After the supine float with flutter kick and the prone float with flutter kick have been learned, it is important to learn to roll from the back to the face and vice versa so that it is not necessary for you to stop swimming in order to take a breath. Start the prone float and flutter kick with your arms out in front. When you wish to roll onto your back, turn your head and draw your shoulder and hip back at the same time. This action will cause you to roll over and you can continue on using the supine float with the flutter kick. To return to the face down position, simply turn your head into one arm and raise your opposite hip and shoulder—you will roll over. If you are still unsuccessful, bring one leg over the other one to complete the turn and go right on kicking. It would help to practice this turning on land before attempting it in the water. When this skill is accomplished your fears should be nearly overcome. (Figure 7.)

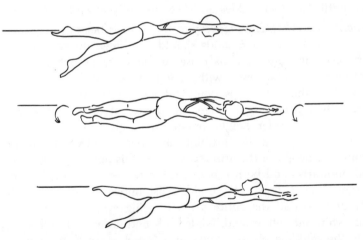

Figure 7—Turning Over From Prone to Supine Positions

ELEMENTARY BACK STROKE

The Stroke—The first stroke you should learn is the elementary back stroke. This is the most practical stroke for beginners because it takes so little effort and breathing is not a problem since the face remains out of the water throughout. Even a novice should be able to go great distances without tiring using this stroke.

The elementary back stroke is basically a three beat rhythm stroke in which your arms and legs work almost simultaneously. The rhythm is (1) *recovery* of both arms and both legs, (2) *power* of both arms and both legs, and (3) *glide* with your body straight and relaxed, but controlled. This stroke is considered a resting stroke because of the long glide phase and the effortless action involved. The key point to remember is that your body should be kept in a straight line without sagging or sitting, particularly during the recovery phase.

The Whip Kick—The most effective kick used with the elementary back stroke is the whip kick. The leg action of this kick is a recovery, power or press, and glide as follows: from the back float position, with ankles extended, your lower legs are dropped from the knees, and your ankles are flexed to a toes-up position and drawn apart so that the knees are pointing inward. There should be no bend at your hips and your feet should be farther apart than the width of your hips at the top of the recovery. Pause at this point to "grab" the water. The bottoms and insides of your feet and lower legs should then press out and around, in one circular motion, until your feet, ankles and legs are fully extended. Glide!

The Arm Stroke—The recovery of the arms is begun just prior to starting the leg recovery. Your hands should be drawn up your sides to your armpits, keeping your arms as close to the body as possible. Both arms are drawn up simultaneously with the elbows in. At this point, your wrists rotate so that the finger tips point out away from your shoulders. Knife your arms to full extension, finger tips first, out to the sides at an angle approximately shoulder height or slightly higher as the legs are being drawn up. Shoulder girdle flexibility and body control in the stroke will determine the height of the arm recovery. At this point the legs have caught up and both arms and both legs begin the power phase of the stroke. Pull your arms directly down to the sides just under the surface with elbows slightly bent so that the entire press is being exerted toward the feet as the legs whip out and around. Glide with both arms and both legs pressed close to the mid-line of your body in a "good posture" position.

At no point throughout the stroke should your arms or legs break the surface of the water. The rhythm should be regular and a long glide (about three seconds), should always be held. The most common errors are: (1) drawing your knees up out of the water rather than dropping your heels down; (2) bending at your hips, which results in a sagging or sitting ac-

tion, rather than keeping the body in good, straight alignment; (3) breaking the *recovery, power, glide* rhythm by not starting your arm recovery
sooner than your leg recovery so that the power of both arms and both
legs is not exerted at the same time, and (4) not always starting and
finishing each complete stroke with a glide. (Figure 8.)

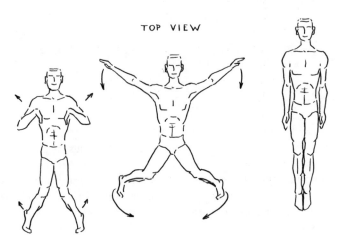

TOP VIEW

Figure 8—Elementary Back Stroke

SURVIVAL SWIMMING

Before you can go on to other forms of swimming, it is necessary to
develop breath control and good breathing habits in the water. Coping
with the unexpected "ducking" or submerging through large waves in the
ocean is done calmly by the swimmer who has command of breath in the
water. You must develop this ability before attempting deep water swimming. (see Chapter 2.)

Progressive Bobbing for Survival—In conjunction with the modified
breast stroke pull and the shallow water bobbing technique that you
learned in Chapter 2, a method of staying afloat and progressing through
the water is easily learned.

Begin practicing this skill in chest deep water and later progress to
deeper water. Take a deep breath and let yourself sink below the surface.
As you go down, let your arms extend forward and to the sides away
from your body. Allow your legs to spread to a forward and back position

How can this swimmer correct his elementary back stroke?

Evaluation Questions

THE ELEMENTARY
BACK STROKE KICK

similar to a wide step. When you are under water press your hands and arms to the sides and down and squeeze your legs together just hard enough to bring your head to the surface. "Grab" a breath of air and let yourself submerge again; exhale gradually. Each time you surface, gasp for some air and slowly exhale as you submerge. Repeat this pattern with the arm and leg action in a regular rhythm, breathing as normally as possible.

Do not thrust too hard on the up stroke of the press and kick, as the farther the head goes above the surface, the deeper you will sink on the next submersion. Time your breathing by using the bobbing technique learned earlier to correspond to the up and down motion of the body. Lean slightly forward as you come up each time to facilitate your progress forward through the water.

Try to relax as much as possible. With practice this technique can be continued for hours and may save your life if you find yourself in a position where you need to stay afloat for an extended period of time. (Figure 9.)

THE CRAWL

The Stroke—The crawl is the stroke best known by people in the United States. This stroke is referred to as "freestyle" in competitive swimming and is presently the fastest stroke man swims. There are several versions but the "American Crawl" is done with one complete arm stroke of both arms to six kicks in each stroke pattern. Your arms pull and recover alternately while your legs execute a continuous up and down "flutter" action. One arm starts the pull or power phase on kick "one" while the other arm is recovered, and the second arm starts the pull or power phase on kick "four"

Diagram B:

THE ELEMENTARY
BACK STROKE KICK

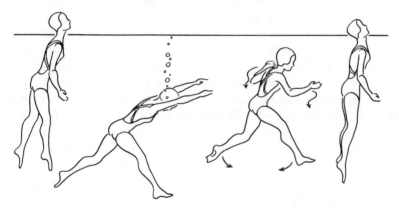

Figure 9—Progressive Bobbing for Survival

while the first arm is recovered. There is no glide phase to this stroke. Some power is exerted throughout.

The Flutter Kick—The flutter kick is used in the crawl stroke, with power exerted in both the up and down press of each leg. You should kick primarily from the hip with your legs nearly straight but relaxed. Your knees should bend slightly, with ankles extended throughout and toes pointed slightly in. Your kick should be an alternating up and down press with a deep but fairly rapid rhythm. Keep your legs and feet entirely under water throughout the kick, with no more than the heel breaking the surface at any time.

21

The Arm Stroke—The arm stroke of the crawl is an alternating pull and recover action with one arm pulling while the other is recovering. Your finger tips should enter the water directly ahead of the shoulder. Fully extend your arm just under the water surface at entry to "grab" the water prior to the pull. Pull your hand and forearm back, close to the mid-line of the body with elbows slightly bent, and then press on through the hip, causing an in-out action, pull-push action. Recover your arm over the water from the hip to the point of entry in front of the shoulder. Neither a tightly bent arm nor a stiff straight arm is desirable on the recovery; a relaxed, rounded arm is the best. As your first arm starts to pull your second arm should be completing its pull and starting its recovery. Continuous pull and recovery action should be incorporated.

The Timing—To execute the total stroke start as in a prone float and flutter kick, with the water level at the hairline, your arms extended out in front, and your body straight. First the kick should be started, then the arm pull should be added and finally the breathing. Take a breath of air by drawing in a short gasp as your head is turned to the side, just far enough to inhale through the mouth. Then turn your face back into the water and gradually exhale with a final spurt just prior to the next inhalation. Your face should be turned toward the pulling arm for the gulp of air just as the pull is being completed, and the face should be turned directly back into the water as the arm starts its recovery. Keep your body in good alignment throughout the stroke with no up and down action or rolling action when your head is turned for the breath. The hairline should be kept at the surface of the water, and the kick should be kept just under the surface with no more than the heel of your foot breaking through at any time. (Figure 10.)

THE BACK CRAWL

The Stroke—The back crawl is racing's back stroke. This is the only competitive swimming stroke done other than in a prone position, and the truly all-around swimmer is always proficient in the back stroke. As in the front crawl, this is done with an alternating pull and recovery arm stroke and continuous "flutter" kick. Your arms are recovered over the water and there should be one complete arm stroke (two arms) to six kicks with one arm pull starting on kick "one" and the second beginning on kick "four." The power of the kick is exerted on the "up" action, and both the arms and the legs are kept nearly straight throughout the stroke. There should be no glide phase in this stroke—action is continuous.

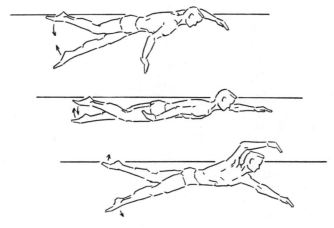

Figure 10—The Crawl Stroke

The Flutter Kick—To start the kick of the back crawl use the same flutter action that was used in the front crawl and strongly emphasize the power or lift in the "up" action as in kicking a football. Keep your ankles extended throughout and your legs should exert power all the way from the hip. To gain maximum force from your kick, each leg must reach *full* extension on the up phase of each alternating up and down kicking action. Your legs and feet should be kept under water throughout the kick, but mounds of water should be raised above the top of the foot on the lift of each leg. Your alternating up and down leg action should be deep but rapid and relaxed.

The Arm Stroke—The alternating pull and recovery action of the arm stroke is similar to that of the crawl stroke. Your finger tips and little finger should enter the water first, almost directly above the shoulder. Knife your hand into the water to "grab" the water prior to the start of the pull. As your hand and forearm are pulled through, keep your elbow bent slightly to pull diagonally under the water at the side of the body with the hand about five to six inches deep. Give a final press at the hips on the last part of your arm stroke. The pull-push action creates a pull all the way from above the shoulder to your hip. Your arm is then recovered over the water, completely straight, from the hip to the entry position, but rotate your wrist on the recovery to permit the finger tips and little finger to enter the water first. As one arm starts the pull the other should be completing its pull and starting its recovery. The pull and recovery action should be continuous without a glide or stop at the side of the body.

What is incorrect about the head position in the breathing phase of this crawl stroke? How should the head look?

Evaluation Questions

HEAD POSITION IN THE CRAWL

The Timing—Start the total back crawl stroke from a back float and flutter kick position with your arms extended overhead, both arms in the water as in the supine float and flutter kick. Add the kick, concentrating on keeping your body in good alignment, ears in the water and chin neither tucked way down nor lifted way up. From this point pull one arm through to the hip thus beginning the arm cycle, and you are on your way. Although breathing is not a problem since the face is maintained above water, it should be as rhythmic and natural as possible. Be sure that your arm is kept straight on the recovery and is not raised over your face or behind your head, but is kept in a diagonal position above the water, and entering above the shoulder. The body should be held in good alignment with no "sitting" or bending sideways, and remember to kick from the hip with a full leg extension on the "up" phase. (Figure 11.)

THE SIDE STROKE

The Stroke—The side stroke is not a competitive swimming stroke, but it is invaluable for life saving purposes. It is also one of the least tiring strokes, since the same muscles are used in the kick as in daily walking.

The side stroke rhythm consists of a pull, one arm pulling while the other arm and both legs recover; a *kick*, the legs press together and the second arm pushes as the first arm recovers; and a *glide*, during which the body is held in straight alignment with one arm extended and the other at the side. Start this *pull, kick* and *push, glide* on your side with both legs together. The arm which is under your body is extended straight out from the shoulder, and the arm that is on top of the body is held at your side. Your head rests on the water with the face turned up so that the back of

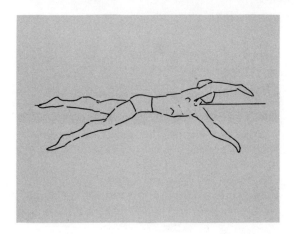

Diagram C:

HEAD POSITION IN
THE CRAWL

your head is on the extended arm. This is the glide position. The extended arm then starts the pull while both legs and your other arm are drawn up in the recovery, at this time the legs are extended forward and back with the top leg moving forward. As the extended arm completes the pull and starts the recovery, your legs are pressed together and at the same time the second arm is pressed down to your side, thus thrusting the body forward with strong power into the glide position. Complete the stroke by holding a long glide.

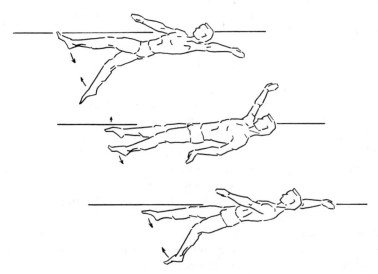

Figure 11—The Back Cráwl Stroke

25

Is this swimmer performing the standard or the inverted scissors kick? Do you know when the inverted kick is the preferred kick?

Evaluation Questions

THE SIDE STROKE KICK

The Scissors Kick—Work on your side stroke equally on both sides and practice no more on one side than the other so that future success can be more easily attained in future equilaterally patterned strokes. This kick is often referred to as the "scissors" kick, for the legs make a scissoring action in exerting power. From the glide position, draw your legs up by bending both the knees and the hips until the hip and knee joints are at approximately forty-five degree angles. Extend your legs forward and back rather than laterally from the hip, with the top leg moving forward and the bottom leg moving back. Your forward ankle should be flexed in a toe-up position and the back ankle should be extended in a toe-pointed position. At this point pause slightly to "grab" the water just prior to the press or power phase, in which your legs are "squeezed" hard together to full leg and ankle extension. This is the most efficient kick to use in the survival bobbing technique described in Chapter 3.

The Arm Stroke—The arm pattern of the side stroke is not particularly powerful but is rather a stabilizing agent for the forceful thrust of the kick, as well as a support for the head. From the glide position pull the lower, extended arm diagonally under the upper body to the chest area with the elbow slightly bent and your finger tips pointing down so that the hand and forearm can be used to attain maximum power. At this point, bend your elbow in tightly to your body while your wrist is rotated to permit the finger tips to knife just under the surface of the water in the recovery back to the glide position. As your extended arm starts the pull, the top arm is drawn up the side of your body and then your finger tips knife diagonally out in front of the chest to start the pull. The top arm push is a short hand and forearm push or press from the chest area down to your hip. Your top

Diagram D:

THE SIDE STROKE KICK

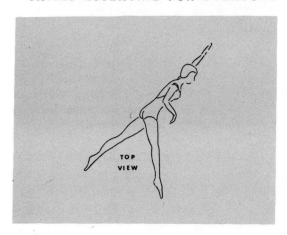

arm and both legs are recovered while the lower arm pulls, and your lower arm is recovered as the top arm and legs exert power. Each complete stroke should be followed by a long glide phase.

The Timing—The side stroke, like any gliding or resting stroke, should be started and finished with a glide. Good body alignment is essential for

Figure 12—The Side Stroke

27

What is wrong with this glide position in the breast stroke?

Evaluation Questions

THE BREAST STROKE
GLIDE

maximum success with a minimum of effort. Your extended arm should be kept just under your head and the surface of the water until the pull is started, and your top arm and both legs should be held tight together until the recovery is started. Lift your head neither up out of the water nor drop it deep into the water, but keep your face turned up so that it is above the surface at all times. Since your face is out of the water, breathing again is not a problem but it should be rhythmic and as normal as possible. Be very certain to work equally hard on each side in the side stroke and be sure that your top leg always stretches forward. (Figure 12.)

THE BREAST STROKE

The Stroke—Another pull, kick, glide stroke, the breast stroke, is done entirely in a prone position, with a simultaneous pull of both arms followed by a simultaneous kick of both legs and a full body extension into a glide. A competitive swimming stroke, the breast stroke has many and varied styles. One fact common to all, however, is parallelism. Both arms and both legs must work simultaneously and remain parallel to each other and to the surface throughout the stroke.

The Whip Kick—Your kick is started with the recovery beginning just as your hands start to pull. Your knees should be bent to a ninety degree angle as your legs are drawn up with the ankles flexed and apart and the knees in close together. There is a slight hesitation at this point to "catch" the water prior to the press. On the kick, press your feet out and back in a circular, whipping action, with the soles and insides of your feet and ankles feeling the greatest resistance. There should be a slight knee

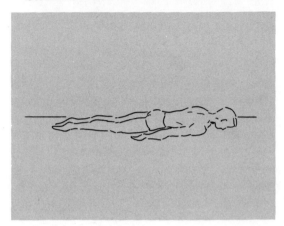

Diagram E:

THE BREAST STROKE
GLIDE

rotation in the power phase. This kick is called the "whip" kick. It is extremely important that your ankles be flexed on the recovery and extended *during* the kick in order to secure the maximum power. Finish your whip kick with a full leg extension to the glide.

The Arms Stroke—Your arm stroke for the breast stroke should be started from an extended position as in a prone float. Draw your hands and forearms diagonally back and down, with the elbows bending on the pull so the hands and forearms can be used as broad paddles. The pull is a short, whipping movement, carried to shoulder level only, with the elbows held high and finger tips diagonally out and down. Then whip your forearms in under the chin, with a final thrust before your recovery, and knife your finger tips close to the surface through the water back to the extended position.

Breathing—Breathing in the breast stroke is added in a *pull* and *inhale, kick, glide* rhythm. Your head should be raised very slightly as the arms start the pull in order to take a short breath of air; then drop your head immediately back into the water and exhale as the power of the kick is being exerted. A final thrust of air should be blown out just prior to a new breathing cycle. As your stroke becomes more efficient, it may be necessary to breathe on alternate, rather than subsequent, strokes.

The Timing—Start the total breast stroke from a prone float position with your face in the water. As the arm pull is started, lift your head up to breathe. Your chin should still be resting on the water. Draw your legs up with feet flexed and apart and knees together; pause prior to the press. As your arms are knifed into the recovery, whip your legs and feet out and down to a fully extended position. Finish your stroke in a full prone glide. (Figure 13.)

Figure 13—The Breast Stroke

JUMPING AND DIVING

It is extremely important that you know the conditions of the water before you enter it. You should never jump into a pool or lake without first knowing the depth, the temperature, and whether or not there is any-one swimming there. A weak swimmer in particular should check the depth. Many times a novice is caught in water just slightly over his head as a result of poor judgment. He should note both the depth and the tempera-ture in order to avoid injury from a too shallow entry, or shock or muscle cramp or tenseness from fear and cold. All swimmers should avoid entry into unknown or dark water or water that is too shallow for jumping or diving. Often the skilled swimmer is prone to carefree play and injuries can result from jumping or diving on other swimmers.

Jumping and Leveling Off—You must learn how to jump into the water, level the body off and proceed into a stroke before you can be considered safe in deep water. The skill should be practiced until the swimmer can jump into water well over his head and surface into a stroke with ease.

When jumping, be sure the area is clear of other swimmers; then step clear of the deck and keep your feet in under your body. In the water, tuck your body with chin in and knees to chest, then extend your legs back and your arms forward to a prone float and flutter kick position. Flutter kick to the surface and swim away. (Figure 14.)

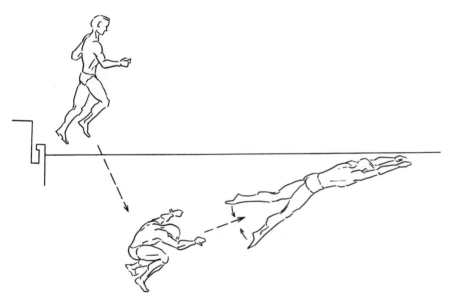

Figure 14—Entering Deep Water and Leveling Off

Deck Diving—From the jump into the water you should progress to a stationary dive into deep water. If you are a beginner you should first kneel on the side of the pool. With the toes of one foot curled over the edge, extend your arms out and down from the shoulders with your head down so that your arms are over your ears. This may also be practiced from water level by sitting on the deck with both feet on the pool gutter. From this position, allow yourself to roll forward, reaching for the bottom of the pool with your finger tips. The most important thing is to keep your arms over your ears and to reach for the bottom of the pool. Do not lift your head to look where you are diving, but lead with the top of your head.

Once the kneeling dive is accomplished, advance to a standing position. Again, with toes curled over the side, bend over with your arms

31

stretched over your ears, as before. Bend down far enough so that the finger tips are pointing toward the bottom of the pool and not out away from you. Keeping arms straight, legs straight, and head down, allow your body to roll forward to enter headfirst, with finger tips reaching for the *bottom* of the pool. When *in* the water, level off, as in the jump. As skill increases, start standing straighter, bending at the waist *as* the body is rolled forward to enter the water, finger tips first. Later a spring may be added to complete the dive from the side of the pool. (Figure 15.)

Figure 15—Deck Diving

4

Better Swimmers
Master These Techniques

Flexibility and well-roundedness are the keys to more advanced techniques. Some techniques are learned for competitive purposes, some for symmetrical body development, some for eventual participation in such activities as life saving, synchronized swimming, speed swimming, SCUBA diving and water polo, and some are learned just for the fun of finding out how much you can do.

SURFACE DIVING

Tuck Surface Dive—Getting under water from a position on the surface of the water is a skill that should be mastered by all participants in water sports. This ability is essential for life saving, SCUBA diving and synchronized swimming and is a major part of any general swimming program. The simplest of the surface dives is the *tuck* surface dive. In this surface dive your legs are tucked up from a prone glide position, with the head held in line with the body. As the arms are pulled back to the hips and then down through the water toward the face, the chin is tucked; the action will cause your tucked body to dive forward. As the arms are almost in line with the face, extend your body so that your legs are stretched toward the sky. The lift of the legs will force your body down toward the bottom of the pool. You should avoid pulling too hard in the tuck position or the head will pass the vertical line and the surface dive will take a sharp angle in under the body rather than straight down.

Pike Surface Dive—The next type of surface dive you should try is done in essentially the same way but you keep your legs straight with the body in a *pike* position. The pike surface dive is started again from

How can this surface dive be corrected?

Evaluation Questions

THE PIKE SURFACE DIVE

the prone glide position. From the prone glide, tuck the chin and pull your arms back to your hips. Then rotate your wrists in order to pull down and through to the face. The body should be piked with the head in line with the body as the arms pull back. The legs should be lifted to the vertical as the arms are drawn from the hip level to the face. It is important that you make the one circular arm pull do the work and avoid tucking the chin to start down, for a tuck of the chin will create the same error of diving in under the body as the over tuck of the body will do in the tuck surface dive. (Figure 16.)

Footfirst and Swim Down Surface Dives—There are two less common dives, the *footfirst* and the *swim down* surface dives. The footfirst surface dive is used in unknown or dark water where the bottom may be dangerous. The swim down surface dive is used for very shallow or fast moving dives such as are often needed in life saving. The footfirst surface dive is started from a vertical position in deep water. Your body is thrust out of the water by exerting a strong scissors or breast stroke kick. As the body starts down after the thrust, your arm pull should be started. Knife your arms down by the sides to the hips and then press up toward the surface in a palms-up pull, forcing the body to dive in a straight line, feet first toward the bottom of the pool. In this dive it is important to keep the body straight and in good alignment.

The swim down surface dive is a simple tuck of the chin from a crawl or any prone position stroke which causes your body to start to drop. As your chin is tucked both arms should be drawn back to the hips as in the tuck and pike surface dives. This action effects a shallow body dive but there is no subsequent lift of the legs, only a hip bend, so the depth that is achieved in the other dives is not accomplished here.

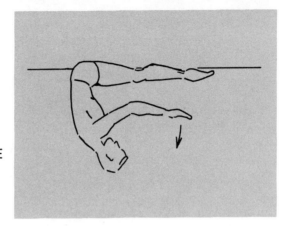

Diagram F:

THE PIKE SURFACE DIVE

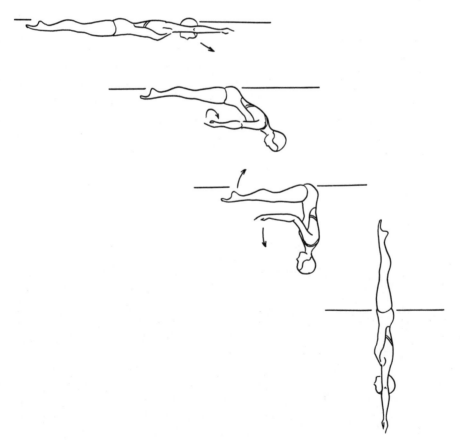

Figure 16—The Pike Surface Dive

Can you surface dive and recover an object in 6 feet of water? in 10 feet? in 15 feet?

Evaluation Questions

TREADING WATER

The skill of treading water is one that all swimmers should master, and it is mandatory for participation in the strenuous sport of water polo. This skill is essential for safety also so that you can maintain yourself in the water after a spill, as in water skiing or boating. Treading water should be a relaxed, efficient action of gently and slowly drawing your hands and forearms back and forth through the water with palms down in a sculling action out from the sides of the body, while your legs gently press in an alternating scissors kick or whip kick action. Only enough effort should be exerted to maintain the face above the surface. No effort should be made to keep the entire head and shoulders up. The most important thing to remember is to RELAX.

DIVING FROM A BOARD

Stationary Diving—The use of a springboard is an entirely different action from diving off a solid surface. Springboard diving should be approached with caution to avoid serious injury. The first step you should take is the dive from a standing position, as was done from the side of the pool. Because of the additional height above the water, you should tuck your chin very slightly and aim farther out, but still reach toward the bottom of the pool with the finger tips. Once you have accomplished the standing dive, a gentle spring may be added. Again, you should be careful not to sharply tuck the chin on the take-off for this will cause your body to flip over or your legs to slap back. Continue diving from a standing position with a minimum spring until control is developed. You should be

Evaluation Questions

Can you tread water for 1 minute? for 2 minutes? for 5 minutes? for 10 minutes?

sure to hold your legs together and straight once you have taken off into the dive, and your arms should be straight and squeezed tightly over the ears on the entry into the water.

The Running Approach—Once the body is well controlled in standing dives, an approach is needed before you can advance to the more difficult

Figure 17—Springboard Diving—The Running Approach

37

How can this diver correct his body alignment?

Evaluation Questions
BODY ALIGNMENT
IN DIVING

categories. A legal approach in competitive diving must have a minimum of four steps. These four steps should be made up of three walking steps and a jump which is called a "hurdle." You can take more steps if you wish, but no less than four. For maximum control, the approach steps should be taken slowly and deliberately; the hurdle should be equal in length to the preliminary steps and should lift the body up rather than forward or backward on the board. The take-off should be an elevating movement, again, *up* rather than *out* off the board. The arms should be controlled throughout the approach and take-off as well as in the dive itself. As the knee is lifted on the hurdle both arms rise, then press to "ride the board" as you jump. Lift your arms again to raise the body forward and up off the board for the take-off into a dive. (Figure 17.)

The Forward Dive in Pike Position—Probably the first dive you should learn is the forward dive in pike position, which is better known as the "jack knife." This dive is the one which best begins the development of body control and awareness of position. It is very important to avoid grabbing for the toes or tucking the chin, for these actions will throw the body well beyond center and cause the same flip over or leg drop action as in surface diving. Try instead to lift your hips above your shoulders into the pike position and draw the feet up to the finger tips rather than your finger tips down to your feet; then look and reach for the bottom of the pool. A final stretch into the water completes the dive. Progressing into other dives is a matter of specific practice, but all dives are successful primarily because of the control and perfection of the approach and the use of the head in the dive itself.

38

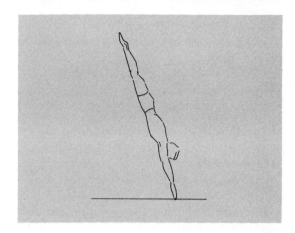

Diagram G:

BODY ALIGNMENT
IN DIVING

INVERTED BREAST STROKE

The Stroke—The inverted breast stroke is probably the most difficult stroke for the average swimmer. Not commonly used, the stroke is employed particularly in life saving and synchronized swimming. It starts in the supine glide position, with the arms stretched overhead. From the arms-extended glide position, pull your arms down to your hips, and as your arms recover, your legs are drawn up to press out and down in the whip kick. The leg press is taken as the arms are stretched overhead in the recovery. Finish the stroke in an arms-overhead, supine glide position.

The Whip Kick—The kick of the inverted breast stroke is the same as the whip kick used in the elementary back stroke. Your lower legs are dropped with heels apart and feet flexed but knees together. From this recovery, the feet are pressed out and around with the bottom and insides of your feet feeling the greatest pressure. Be sure the whip action is out and around all in one motion. Glide, with your feet together and your legs straight.

The Arm Stroke—The arm pull differs from other strokes in that the pull is taken from the full arm extension overhead to the hips, effecting a pull all the way to the hips. The arm recovery from the hips to approximately the shoulders occurs before the recovery kick is started. In this part of the recovery your arms should be kept as close to the body as possible. Your arms are then stretched overhead as the power of the kick is exerted. Complete your stroke in an arms-overhead glide.

Breathing—Breathing should not be a problem, for again the face should be above the surface at all times, but the most effective breathing

39

action is an inhalation on the pull and an exhalation on the kick. A slight alternate tucking and dropping back of the head adds to the efficiency and fluidity of the stroke. As the pull is taken bring your head slightly forward into a chin tucked position, and as the whip of your kick is exerted drop your head slightly back, in a chin up position, to stretch into the glide.

The Timing—The timing of the inverted breast stroke is not difficult if you think of starting and finishing each stroke in a glide position with arms overhead. You may have some trouble keeping the face above the surface at first, a difficulty which is usually a result of drawing your knees up too high on the recovery of your kick or "sitting" in the water, but smoothing out the other parts of the stroke will help you correct these faults. This is sometimes called the "dip and dive" stroke. Its perfection is simple if the correct technique is used. (Figure 18.)

TOP VIEW

Figure 18—The Inverted Breast Stroke

BUTTERFLY STROKE

The Stroke—This stroke is not one of the accepted nine styles of swimming, but it is one of the competitive strokes used in all aspects of swimming competition. The stroke has become the second fastest stroke known, but because of its extreme difficulty it is not perfected by many noncompetitive swimmers. As it probably is the most exhausting form of swimming one must be in excellent condition to perform it for any length of time.

The Dolphin Kick—The most common rhythm of the butterfly stroke is two kicks to one complete arm stroke. There is a major kick as the arm pull is started and a minor kick as the arm recovery is started. Actually the two kicks would be the same but for the fact that the force needed to lift the arms over the water causes one kick to press deeper, thus giving an appearance of an alternation between major and minor kicking action. Your kick should be a full body press from a pike to an arch at the hips, followed by a continuous up and down press of the knees, ankles and feet. Your legs and feet must be parallel to each other throughout the kick. Equal power should be exerted both up and down in each kick.

The Arm Stroke—The arm stroke is a double arm pull and over-the-water recovery, with simultaneous arm action throughout. Your hands should knife into the water, finger tips first, in front of the shoulders. Both hands and forearms are then pulled back, with elbows bent, close to the midline of the body, to just under the chest. A second pressing or pushing action is then taken from the chest to an out of the water position at the hips. This *pull-push* action effects an "s" or in-out power phase of your arm stroke. Recover your arms simultaneously over the water to knife again into the entry in front of the shoulders. There is no glide taken in this stroke for arm action is continuous.

Breathing—Breathing in the butterfly stroke is, and must be a conscious effort in order to maintain the consistent stroke rhythm. Often your head is raised too soon or too late which causes an up and down motion in the stroke rather than a smooth, gliding forward motion. Just as in the breast stroke, your head should be lifted slightly as the arm pull is started to gasp a breath of air. Drop your head back into the water as the back press of the arm stroke is taken. Exhale under water, with a final out thrust just prior to the next breath. Your head may be lifted directly forward or to the side for breathing provided your shoulders are held squarely parallel to the surface.

The Timing—Counting a kick on the down beat, the total rhythm of the butterfly stroke is a *pull-kick-kick* or down kick of the legs at the end of the first "pulling" part of the arm stroke and a second down kick of the legs on the final "pressing" arm action, up out of the water to the recovery.

41

You might think of this sequence as a kick as you start the pull and a kick as you start the recovery. (Figure 19.)

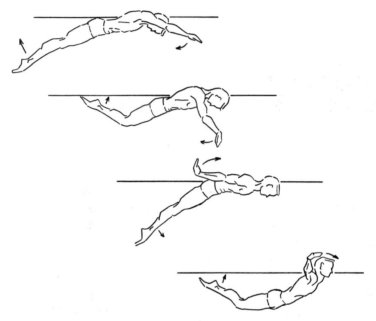

Figure 19—The Butterfly Stroke

5

Progress
Can Be Speeded Up

Swimming, like most sport activities, is complicated and certainly one needs many hours of practice to perfect the various strokes. For most rapid learning, you should take advantage of a course taught by a qualified instructor. Learning by yourself or copying others is not only difficult but may lead to bad habits that are hard to break when you later want to learn correctly.

In addition to the expert instruction which a qualified teacher can provide, regular practice sessions are required. Distributed practice is superior to massed practice when learning complicated skills that require long periods of time to master. The two or three times per week that your class meets helps to provide this arrangement. In addition to the class time you will probably have to do a little homework on your own to progress at your most rapid rate.

When in class, pay attention to what the instructor says and make every effort to do as he indicates. He has taught many people to swim and has found certain techniques that help beginners learn quickly. When you practice on your own time, don't just play in the water. Work on the specific points that were mentioned in class. Do some of the drills and exercises that you know will help you. Remember that it will take a conscious effort to overcome fears and to learn new skills such as rhythmic breathing and coordinated movements of the arms, legs, and head. Mere exposure to the water and horseplay with friends will not teach you how to swim.

Understanding the scientific reasons for the particular movements of the strokes will help you learn and remember the proper technique. Students

Can you swim the crawl stroke 10 yards? 25 yards? 50 yards?

Evaluation Questions

frequently ask, "Why it is more tiring to swim the crawl stroke by raising my head up to breathe rather than turning it to the side?" With an understanding of Archimedes' principle of buoyancy when an object is submerged in a medium, such a question can be partly answered. As long as the head is submerged, the water exerts a buoyant force upward equal to the weight of the water displaced by the head. By turning it to the side to breathe, you can take advantage of some of this force even while your nose and mouth are out of the water. Lifting it completely out of the water removes the force and the entire weight of the head presses the body deeper into the water. The same reasoning applies to performing a "ballet leg" in synchronized swimming. While the leg is under water, it is buoyed up by a force equal to the weight of the water it displaces. As soon as you lift it up, the buoyancy is gone and the weight of the leg presses you down. You can also take advantage of this weight by forcing your legs high into the air when performing a surface dive.

In addition to losing the buoyant force when you lift your head up to breathe, such action causes an arch in your back that tends to lower your hips and legs. This position in the water presents a greater surface area (neck and chest) to the water and slows you down. Have you ever tried to push a kickboard broadside through the water? Compare this feeling with pushing it horizontally with the water. The science of kinesiology helps us understand this and other principles related to the movement of the human body in air and water.

Applying Newton's Third Law of Motion, action and reaction, may help you develop better technique in developing the driving force in the arm pull or the kick of various strokes. By forcing the water in one direction (toward the feet) the body is propelled head first through the water. Force is opposite to the direction of movement. Ask your teacher for a more detailed analysis of this and other physical laws that govern swimming strokes. By understanding these principles and putting them to use, you will learn faster and become a more efficient swimmer.

When you have mastered the techniques of the various strokes you will want to develop some speed and endurance in the water. To develop your speed, correct technique plus forcing yourself to swim fast for 25 or 50 yards is required. Swim repeat 50's with about 30 seconds rest between each one. Start with two, then build to three, four, even ten in a row.

To develop endurance, aim at being able to swim 440 yards. Start with 100 yards and increase the distance by 25 or 50 yards each week. Be sure to utilize correct breathing and body position. Minimize any extreme motion such as too much body roll, movement of the trunk back and forth sideways, or excessive head action. Relax and change strokes occasionally in order to utilize different muscle groups. Force yourself to keep going when you begin to get tired. Your cardiovascular system can't improve unless you make it work. Once you have made a quarter of a mile, the half and full mile are easy. If you would like to enter competitive swimming, see a coach for more specific workout schedules or have your teacher set up a workout plan for you.

6

Patterns of Play

Swimming is fun and there are interesting and exciting things to do in the water regardless of your level of skill, provided you practice those safety factors which must be observed and know your own skill and strength limitations. Drownings usually occur as a result of unwise decisions or an overestimation of ability. After you have accurately evaluated your swimming ability, select those activities suited to your interest and personality.

KINDS OF ACTIVITIES

All ages enjoy floatation devices for leisurely or spirited play around a home pool. Anything from an old inner tube to a styrofoam kickboard or tub is adequate support for water tag, races or contests. Beach balls are great fun to dodge, pass, or shoot for corners or goals while the opposing team defends them. Diving for pennies, stones or rubber bricks is also fun but be careful when playing in a crowded pool, and never leave them sitting on the bottom when you are finished. Each pool situation will govern the rules of play.

Beach Swimming—Another type of water activity is found at the beach; and a wide variety of games are played there. One must *learn* to have fun at the beach, however. Many people avoid swimming at the beach because "the waves are too rough," when actually they just don't know how to enjoy them. When first learning about ocean or lake swimming, you should start slowly, in waist deep water, jumping gentle waves while turning to "give with the wave" rather than standing fast and resisting them. After the feeling of "giving" with the wave is established, then try diving in under the wave. Just before the wave breaks, take a shallow dive right into it. Start by diving through light waves, for a stronger wave may tumble you over. Even a strong swimmer should be aware of danger signals and restricted areas at beaches. When storm warnings, undertow or other restrictions are posted, *observe them!*

In addition to wave jumping or wave diving at the beach, it is fun to glide with the surf. Body surfing requires only a small wave. Beginning body surfers may choose to use a styrofoam float board to help them along, but no *air filled* floatative devices should ever be used at a beach. Board surfing is a great sport, and it has become so popular in some places that special surfing sites have been established where swimming is not permitted. All kinds of surfing are basically the same. The surfer must try to "catch" a wave by swimming hard just as it approaches him and then either stretching his body or lying flat on the board to "ride" the wave into shore. Board surfers later can learn to do all kinds of exciting moves and tricks on their boards.

Competitive Swimming and Diving—Other water activities include many varieties of sports and games. The racing enthusiast may choose to enter competitive swimming through the local A.A.U., swim school, YMCA, or club. In competitive swimming one may enter any of several events. The strokes included are the butterfly, the back stroke, the breast stroke, and freestyle. Competitive swimming does not incorporate any of the other strokes except in a form swimming category. One may choose to swim any or all of these strokes in either sprints (short races) or distance (long races), or become an all around swimmer and compete in the individual medley which is a race in which each swimmer performs each of the four strokes.

The person who is concerned with control rather than speed may choose to participate in springboard diving, form swimming or synchronized swimming. In each of these instances, the body must be in good form and controlled throughout the execution of a stroke, stunt or dive in order to win an event. Each of these activities is judged by a panel of experts and the diver, swimmer or synchronized swimmer is awarded points according to the dive, stroke or stunt difficulty and the perfection of its execution. After each of the participants has performed the required number of dives, strokes or stunts to the best of his ability, a winner is determined based on the maximum total of scores given times the point difficulty.

Can you swim 440 yards? Can you swim it under 12 minutes? 10 minutes? 8 minutes?

Evaluation Questions

Skin And Scuba Diving—If you are a natural adventurer, you are probably interested in either skin or SCUBA diving. Both skin and SCUBA diving should be learned in a pool rather than in a lake or an ocean. In skin diving, the swimmer wears only a diving mask, flippers and a snorkle. This form of diving limits his capacity to stay under water and the extent to which he can explore the bottom of the swimming area. But the real sportsman prefers the challenge of outwitting a fish with his natural breath control. Many others prefer skin diving for underwater exploration because the equipment is less expensive and less cumbersome than SCUBA gear.

In SCUBA diving the swimmer is assisted in his ability to stay under water by a diving tank strapped to his back. If deep or cold water SCUBA diving is engaged in, "wet suits" are also usually worn. Neither of these activities, particularly SCUBA diving, should be entered into lightly or with limited instruction. Knowledge and experience are essential to safety in the use of diving equipment, and instruction in the diving area, its currents, depths and living creatures should be well established before a novice skin or SCUBA diver enters the water. If caution and understanding are assured, both skin and SCUBA diving are exciting, exhilarating activities.

Water Polo—The team oriented sportsman will most certainly enjoy the sport of water polo, but only a very strong swimmer can endure the rigors of this game. The fact that it is normally played in deep water and the requirement that as a player you must have your feet off the bottom while playing the ball make water polo strenuous exercise. Only modified versions of this game can be played in home pools, for the required depth and size are not common to them, and the official goals are cumbersome and require fittings in the pool deck. But whether it is played as a home version or as a competitive team sport, it is fun to develop the skills of passing the ball without touching the bottom and trying to score by getting the ball into the goal which is defended by your opponents.

Other water sports and games require a limited to comprehensive knowledge of swimming and are both fun and beneficial. Some of these are water skiing, boating, canoeing, sailing, aqua planing, and numerous others, but none of these water sports or games should be taken lightly. Knowledge and ability in basic swimming skills and the use of protective devices such as life jackets are a "must" to insure maximum safety, and only an experienced person should handle the boat or canoe.

Swimming, water games and sports are fun, healthful and exhilarating if entered into wisely. The greater your understanding of all aspects of water skills, the greater potential you have for fun. Develop your skill and your understanding of swimming and the water for your maximum safety and enjoyment.

7

Language and Lore of Swimming

Man probably learned how to swim from watching animals; however, the origin of swimming really is not known. Mosaics unearthed in Pompeii show men navigating water under their own power, and a bas-relief in a tomb from the 2000 B.C. period in Egypt shows a swimmer doing what appears to be a crawl stroke. The word "swimming" is derived from the old English term "swimmin."

The English were the first people of modern times to compete in swimming as a sport rather than using it primarily as a skill for survival. Records show that competitive swimming began about 1837 in London. Early English swimmers used the breast stroke and the side stroke.

In 1844 North American Indians entered a swimming meet in London. "Flying Gull defeated Tobacco by swimming the length of a 130-foot pool in 30 seconds." The style of swimming used by the Indians was similar to a windmill action. Each arm thrashed the water violently in circles, while the feet beat the water in an up and down action. This type of action was later known as the crawl stroke.

Most early swimming consisted primarily of the breast stroke and some side stroking. In the late 1800's, J. Arthur Trudgen introduced an overhand stroke using the scissor kick which was to become known as the "trudgen crawl." Using the trudgen crawl, J. H. Derbyshire swam 100 yards in 60 seconds for the world record. This stroke has recently been restored to competitive swimming, and some modern distance swimmers have set new records using it.

In 1878, Frederick Cavill, an Englishman, went to Australia. After observing that the natives' leg action resulted in exceptional speed, he combined it with the double overhand stroke. This stroke became known as the "Australian crawl." About 1905, Charles M. Daniels, a swimmer for the New York Athletic Club, introduced the "American crawl" and used it to set a world record of 54.8 seconds in the 100 yard swim in 1910. The only difference between the "Australian crawl" and the "American crawl" was that in the American crawl the kick was timed to the stroking of the arms—six beats of the legs for every revolution of the arms.

Glossary of Terms

The following definitions may be helpful to you in understanding the terminology of water sports.

1. Approach and hurdle—the walking steps (approach) and the jump (hurdle) to the end of the springboard in diving. The approach must contain at least three steps. The hurdle consists of lifting one leg up until the thigh is parallel to the board and the lower leg is perpendicular to the board, jumping off of the other foot and landing on both feet.

2. Archimedes' principle—an object immersed in a medium is buoyed up by a force equal to the weight of the volume of the medium displaced. Usually the medium is water, but it could be any liquid or gas. A balloon floats in air because it weighs less than the volume of the air it displaces. Your body floats in water because you weigh less than the water you displace. If you cannot float, then you weigh more than the water you displace.

3. Butterfly—a relatively new stroke, used in competition and considered the second fastest stroke. The arms work in a crawl action but both hit the water and pull at the same time. The kick is a dolphin kick similar to the flutter, but both feet kick up and down together at the same time.

4. Finning—an action of the arms like the fins of a fish, resulting mostly from the movement of the elbow and the wrist in and out from the body, in a press and recovery action.

5. Float—to be suspended in the water.
   a. jellyfish float—to float with your arms and legs hanging down in the water, hands holding ankles, head down in water, and your rounded back bobbing above the surface.
   b. prone float—to float face down with arms and legs extended.
   c. supine float—to float face up with arms and legs extended.

6. Glide—the resting phase of the breast, elementary back and side stroke. The body is floating and gliding through the water as a result of the last kick and pull of the arms. The glide usually is held for two or three seconds.

7. Gutter—the edge of the pool at water level. Water from the surface splashes over the gutter and is drained away.

8. Kick—to propel the body through the water with the legs.
   a. dolphin—both legs moving up and down together.
   b. flutter—both legs moving up and down alternately.
   c. frog—a bending and outward movement of the knees with the heels together and toes pointed out, extension of the knees, and squeeze of the legs together to a stretch position. The action follows a 1, 2, 3 count described as up, apart, together, with all phases having equal time. The legs extend laterally to the body.
   d. scissors—a bending of the knees and extension of the legs forward and backward in relation to the body, than a hard squeeze to a stretch position. Probably the most powerful but not the fastest kick. While lying on the side in the water, if the top leg extends forward it is called the regular scissors kick, but if the top leg extends backward it is called the inverted scissors kick. The inverted kick is used only in certain lifesaving techniques.
   e. wedge—similar to the frog, except that the knees and feet are both drawn apart as the knees bend, with the circular press and extension of the whip kick. The 1, 2, 3 timing is also similar to the whip kick.
   f. whip—similar to the frog, but as the knees bend the heels and toes are both farther to the side than the knees which are held close together. The feet then whip around in a circle to a stretch position. In the up, apart, squeeze action, the last two actions receive as much time as the first one by itself.

9. Pike—a body position with the knees straight, the hips bent and the back straight. The arms may be holding the legs or extended out to the side.

10. Hurdle—see approach and hurdle.

11. Pull—an action of the arms by pulling the water toward the body.

12. Push—an action of the arms or legs by pushing the water away from the body.

13. Recovery phase—the part of a stroke in which the arms or legs have thrust the body through the water and are now returning to the position for another thrust.

14. SCUBA—Self-Contained Underwater Breathing Apparatus. Usually an air tank strapped to the back and connected to the mouth by a flexible tube and mouthpiece.

15. Sculling—a means of propelling oneself through the water with the hands and forearms executing an in and out action. Pressure is being exerted on both the in and out phases of the arm action.

16. Skin dive—to explore and dive in water using only a face mask, a snorkle tube, and swim fins.

17. Snorkle tube—a tube, usually about a foot long going from the mouth to just above the surface of the water. The swimmer breathes through the tube.

18. Stretch—to extend the body into a straight line with arms and legs extended, toes pointed, and back straight.

19. Stroke—a complete cycle of the arms and legs in a coordinated manner. Sometimes this term refers only to the arm action of the total movement.

20. Surfing—to swim with the waves at the beach and let them carry you to the shore. Board surfing consists of standing, kneeling, or sitting on a long board and riding the waves to shore.

21. Synchronized swimming—a form of swimming using various strokes and water stunts to music. Many of the stunts are extremely difficult to accomplish. The competitors are judged on their form, style, originality, and the difficulty of the moves.

22. Tuck—a body position with the knees bent, the hips bent, and the chest on the knees. The hands are usually holding on to the shinbones. The head may be forward or backward.

23. Water ski—to stand on one or two boards about five feet long and six to eight inches wide and be pulled over the water by a boat. The skis have rubber binding to hold your feet to the boards.

8

Rules of Swimming

The general rules of swimming are concerned mostly with the safety of the participants. Most pools and public swimming areas post regulations which are designed to protect the swimmers. Observation of these rules may be neglected by swimmers because they do not understand the reasons for their existence. It therefore is hoped that clarification of the "whys" of these rules might serve to improve both your interest in and willingness to observe them.

Of the swimming in itself:

1. Never swim alone, regardless of your skill or experience.

    Why? That one time you are alone is when you might get a cramp, slip, be knocked unconscious or meet with some unexpected problem that you cannot solve alone or which keeps you from seeking necessary assistance. It is just common sense to have a buddy while swimming.

2. Do not overestimate your ability.

    Why? Someone dares you to swim to an island in the middle of the lake. You are a strong swimmer, but when an unexpected storm comes up the waves are too much for you, and once you get out there, you are too tired to get back. On the other hand that one last wave you want to "catch" while surfing is just the time *you* get caught. There is always another day to surf, and that little added safety factor of swimming long distances with a boat may keep you alive to do it again. The experts at channel swimming use a boat for their own safety after years of conditioning. You certainly should do the same.

3. Never depend on air filled flotation devices.

   Why? Deep water swimming should be done by capable swimmers or under strict observation by an instructor while learning, and if you are not able to take care of yourself under all unexpected circumstances, stay in the shallow area. Dependence on an air filled inner tube or plastic float is just asking for trouble.

4. Avoid strenuous swimming after eating.

   Why? Obviously a small snack such as a candy bar or hot dog will not affect your system greatly, but you should not enter into strenuous exercises of any kind right after eating a full meal. It would be just as dangerous for you to play a strenuous tennis match or run in a track meet immediately after eating as it would be for you to swim. The only additional factor is that it is more dangerous to get a cramp in the water and the cold of the water contributes to potential cramping of the muscles of the abdomen.

5. Observe regulations involving limitations in swimming areas.

   Why? Lakes and oceans are marked with buoys, to limit the safe swimming areas, by experts who have screened the currents, undertows and marine life that may be harmful. Obviously, anyone who has ever been stung by a Man-of-War in the surf off the Florida coast will be certain to observe the signs a second time. Additionally, the novice who has been caught in the kelp will stay out of that area, but being caught in overwhelming waves or currents might not let you have a second chance. Stay in the swimming area provided!

Around the swimming area:

1. Always look before you jump or dive into a pool.

   Why? Of course none of us want to jump on anyone and diving on someone might prove fatal, but in addition to this factor, it is terribly annoying to a beginner or an older person to be splashed or dunked as a result of horse play. Common courtesy is the key factor in this case.

2. Only one diver on the board at one time.

   Why? It is lots of fun to break the spring of a friend who is about to take off into a "Cannonball" causing him to land a little hard,

Do you know the rules of pool safety? What are they?

but if you stand on the board when a novice is diving he might land flat on his back and injure himself severely. You do not really want to do that, do you? Do not take any chances; you would never forgive yourself if a friend of yours was severely injured as a result of your horseplay.

3. No running on the pool deck.

   Why? This one should be obvious. The pool deck is slippery when wet.

4. Shower before entering the pool.

   Why? Here the concern is more for cleanliness and common decency than safety. The major factor is to remove heavy oils like suntan lotion, greasy hair oil and/or sand and dirt off your suit if you have been playing ball or sunning yourself. With many, many people swimming, the pool can get pretty greasy and dirty if this rule is not observed.

There is one final rule that should be observed by all people: *never attempt a swimming rescue when you are not qualified to do so,* and if you are a qualified lifeguard, swim after someone in distress only when there is *no other means* by which to give assistance. Time and time again we read this kind of headline in the daily newspaper: "Father Drowns Attempting to Save Son," "Two Men Die Rescuing Woman in Flood," etc. How can this be prevented? Certainly a father cannot stand by idly while his son drowns! Naturally not, but there are many other things that can be done other than swimming after the person. Two drownings are never better than one, and if you are not qualified, do not swim out to give assistance. Learn and practice this list instead:

1. Get a pole or broom or anything to extend your reach and assist that way. Make a rope out of clothing, towels, etc., to extend the distance if the pole is not long enough. Once sufficient extension is secured, be certain that your base of support is low and firm so that you are not pulled in the water.

   Why? It takes much less time to gather extensions than it does to swim out, and if you have swum out too fast you will probably be too tired to be of any assistance once you get there. In addition, the fear factor would contribute to your ineffectiveness and rapid exhaustion.

2. Wade out in shallow water to reach an extension to a person in distress. If you cannot reach him alone, form a "human chain" by linking wrists with others until you you can reach him or move out far enough to toss an extension to him. Again, be absolutely certain that the base of support is firm.

   Why? Just as before, assist without endangering yourself as well as the victim.

3. Use a boat if available.

   Why? It is faster and safer for both victim and rescuer.

4. Swim out *with a buoy* or any flotation device and keep it well away from you when you extend it to the victim. Keep him an arm's distance away so that you can freely swim back with him holding onto the buoy.

   Why? Fear can make people do strange things, and being caught in a strangle hold is difficult even for a qualified lifeguard. It might prove fatal to you! Additionally, the flotation device can help support both of you as you move towards safety.

5. Never swim out to assist when you are not qualified.

   Why? You are *not* qualified. Send for someone who is.

Safety in swimming is vital to existence. Don't take unnecessary chances. If someone is in danger, *send for help immediately*. Do not try to be a hero and sacrifice yourself in the process. Swimming can and should be safe and great fun if these few rules are observed.

9

Unwritten Laws

The courtesies and concerns of the swimmer date back to ancient times. Both the Greeks and the Romans participated in swimming. The uncovered ruins of the temple of Agamemnon show that the Greeks even used an overarm stroke similar to today's front crawl, and their concerns were with personal safety just as ours are today. There is evidence that air filled skins similar to our life vests were used for support, and that the Greeks avoided swimming when they were overheated from strenuous physical exercise. These and other traditions were developed from experience and from concern for personal safety and comfort.

In addition to these ancient ideas, modern swimming for leisure, exercise and exhilaration requires other courtesies and safety considerations. Most of these unwritten laws have been established on the principle of doing unto others as you would have done unto you. The unaware showoff who takes a flying leap into a "cannonball" to splash a group of girls and swamps the fully clothed passerby; and the boy who ducks a novice swimmer, at the very least, should be banned from the swimming area. Another problem is the pair of fun lovers who push a girl in before they discover that she can't swim, or this same pair who catch a girl by her hands and feet and swing her back and forth before throwing her in. If one lets go too soon, the result may be serious injury to the girl. This kind of beach and pool play is dangerous and stupid. Discourteous at best, it can result in serious injury or even drowning.

As swimming becomes more popular and beaches and pools become more crowded additional rules requiring consideration for others must be observed. The thoughtlessness of running past sunbathers, showering them

58

with sand, or allowing your pet to do the same, is unkind. Littering the beach or pool deck with bottles, food scraps and the like, is again inconsiderate, and leaving showers, restrooms and dressing rooms clean and uncluttered should be common practice, but often is not.

Care should also be taken in the pool or lake so that you do not swim aimlessly into people. Check behind you before you push off into a backstroke, and always look before you dive. When surfing, you should be concerned with staying well out of the swimming area, and you should avoid cutting out another surfer. Similarly, avoid "cutting in" a line waiting to use the diving board or to buy refreshments. If you are a skilled swimmer, be aware of the less skilled nearby and swim around them so that they are not ducked by your passage. Most organized swimming areas post rules such as these for your personal safety; they should all be stringently observed. And, posted or not, do not: (1) swim alone, (2) swim immediately after eating, (3) swim under the diving boards, (4) run on the pool deck or (5) jump or dive without first checking for other swimmers and the pool depth. In addition always: (1) swim where there is qualified supervision, (2) observe all posted rules and regulations and (3) observe personal hygiene and health guides such as showering before entering the pool.

Swimming is one of the oldest sport forms and one of the first sports practiced as a leisure activity, but the water has always presented some element of fear to man. Common courtesies must be observed where men swim, or that fear element can become so great that the leisure and benefits are lost to those who fear the most.

10

Opportunities Unlimited

There are opportunities galore for participation, observation, instruction, or whatever you wish in the field of aquatics. These opportunities extend from basic swimming, through skin and SCUBA diving, to all forms of boating, canoeing and surfing. No matter what your interest, there are many schools for instruction, clubs and Y's for participation, local and national meets and contests for competition.

Probably the most widespread and varied program in aquatics is headed by the American National Red Cross. This organization has branches in most large cities throughout the nation and each of these branches offers such aquatic activities as water safety instructor courses, life saving junior and senior courses, basic swimming and diving courses, and canoeing, boating and first aid courses with well qualified instructors. This organization also sponsors and directs various aquatic schools throughout the country. These schools provide two week courses for the improvement of all forms of aquatics; enthusiasts are welcome and encouraged to attend. To participate in any of these activities simply contact your local Red Cross for information.

Other extensive instructional programs in swimming are offered regularly by the local chapters of the Young Men's Christian Association and the Young Women's Christian Association, (Y.M.C.A.) and Y.W.C.A.). These programs also are well organized and give good instruction, but are less extensive than the Red Cross programs. Most often these programs are limited to basic swimming.

Competitive programs are usually directed and governed by the Amateur Athletic Union. This governing body establishes the rules of competition for all areas of swimming including synchronized swimming, diving, and water polo. Each competitor who represents the United States in aquatics in the Olympic Games must be a member of the Amateur Athletic Union. The local and national organizations in each specific area of aquatics seek sponsors and organize the meets and contests. For information regarding membership or participation in A.A.U. sponsored events, contact can be made locally or information can be gathered from the rule books which are published annually by the national organization of the Amateur Athletic Union.

Some less familiar organizations offer numerous aquatic activities. One of these is the Women's National Aquatic Forum which is held annually in December at Pompano Beach, Florida. This organization is designed for teachers of aquatics. All areas of aquatics are discussed and demonstrated in order to update and expand ideas in the field. Similarly, the Men's Swim Forum in Fort Lauderdale, Florida, is held at the same time annually, and features the collegiate East-West Swimming meet. The governing body of competitive aquatic sports for high school and college men is determined by the athletic conference in which the school or college is involved. For high school and college competition for women, the Division of Girls and Women's Sports, (D.G.W.S.), of the American Association for Health, Physical Education and Recreation, (A.A.H.P.E.R.), establishes the standards and rules.

In addition to the national and local organizations, there are countless private clubs, swim schools, athletic clubs and recreation centers which offer instruction in all forms of swimming and sponsor many types of competitive teams, such as swimming, diving, synchronized swimming and water polo teams. These club-sponsored teams range from very famous groups like the Santa Clara Swim Club or the Los Angeles Athletic Club, which have contributed many Olympic Champions in swimming and diving, and the San Francisco Merionettes and the University Club which have given us many of the National Champions in synchronized swimming, to the unknown but eager swim school around the corner, which had fifty children entered in the last age-group swim meet.

There is an aquatics activity designed for everyone, and there are thousands of water sports areas throughout the nation. Investigate the opportunities in your locale, then participate in these very healthful and rewarding activities.

61